The Lord's Word is
ours?

[♡ Y0-DOM-181]

Enjoy Karen Callentine

Eph 6:17

Lesson Plans For Life

Kay Kevan Callentine

WestBow
PRESS®
A DIVISION OF THOMAS NELSON
& ZONDERVAN

Scripture taken from the New King James Version. Copyright © 1979, 1980,
1982 by Thomas Nelson, Inc. Used by permission. All rights reserved.

Scripture taken from the King James Version of the Bible.

Scripture taken from the *Amplified Bible*, copyright © 1954, 1958, 1962,
1964, 1965, 1987 by The Lockman Foundation. Used by permission.

WestBow Press books may be ordered through booksellers or by contacting:

WestBow Press
A Division of Thomas Nelson & Zondervan
1663 Liberty Drive
Bloomington, IN 47403
www.westbowpress.com
1 (866) 928-1240

Because of the dynamic nature of the Internet, any web addresses or
links contained in this book may have changed since publication and
may no longer be valid. The views expressed in this work are solely those
of the author and do not necessarily reflect the views of the publisher,
and the publisher hereby disclaims any responsibility for them.

Any people depicted in stock imagery provided by Thinkstock are models,
and such images are being used for illustrative purposes only.
Certain stock imagery © Thinkstock.

ISBN: 978-1-5127-2641-1 (sc)
ISBN: 978-1-5127-2640-4 (e)

Library of Congress Control Number: 2016900406

Print information available on the last page.

WestBow Press rev. date: 01/25/2016

Preface

This book is one my dad never got to read because I kept "putting it off" and he went home to be with the Lord before I "got around to it." It is the encouragement my dad always gave me that makes it possible for me to finish it now. The format of the book comes from my years as a high school teacher. The theme "Red Letter Edition," used by my pastor for year of studying the words of Jesus, added further inspiration for this book. As I studied the words of Jesus in the New Testament they spoke to my heart as I hope this work in the Word of God will speak to yours. It is through a closer walk with the Lord that we find the peace only He can give. May God bless your reading of His Word.

Acts 20:35b (New King James Version) "And remember the words of the Lord Jesus, that He said, 'It is more blessed to give than to receive.'"

Kay Kevan Callentine

Introduction

The Bible is the unfailing Word of God spoken to men and recorded for all generations. It is read by Christians and non-Christians but not with the same impact or for the same reasons. It has been studied by students and scholars and debated by the wise and the foolish. But as the Holy Spirit leads it never returns void (Isaiah 55:11 KJV) nor leaves us without refreshment.

As we read and study the Word of God our lives are changed. Some are dramatically transformed while others are gradually manipulated into Spirit-filled responses. Some of us take for granted the availability of a Bible, having many surrounding us in our homes and churches. The Bible has been translated from the original Hebrew (Old Testament) and Greek (New Testament) into many languages used on earth today. Unfortunately, not every group of people has the Bible in their own language but the work of translation continues. And as the Bible is read and digested, discussed and explained the lives of people are conformed to His will (Romans 8:29 and Romans 12:2).

This devotional is the result of one aspect of God's leading in my life. As the Word has been preached and I have read and studied the Word of God He has provided insights that are shared in this work. May His Word provide refreshment for your soul and guidance for your walk with Him each day.

A Servant's Heart

Topic of the day: servant

Definition: one who works for or is in subjection to another

Words from the scriptures:

Luke 10:38-42
John 13:4-5
John 13:15-17

Example of Jesus:

Luke 22:26-27

Daily meditation:

Resentment causes us to be impotent in the Lord's service. Yet it creeps into our lives because we take our eyes off of our Lord. We don't share the servant's heart attitude Christ set as an example for us to follow. We see ourselves as more important than others. We choose who to encourage and who to support. We reject those we do not deem worthy of our attention. We become complainers like Martha (Luke 10:40-42) when things aren't going our way.

Other Christians and non-Christians observe our behaviors; they listen to our words and they ask themselves what's the difference between these Christians and the rest of the world? We fail to demonstrate the servant model Christ set for us and there is sometimes nothing at all different about us as Christians and the world around us. We've been paralyzed in our witness by our own worldliness and have ceased following our Example. Let us re-examine our testimonies and put resentment out of our lives that we may return to effectiveness for Christ's sake. Let us adopt anew that servant's heart Christ showed us and follow it always.

Prayer of my heart:

Loving Lord, guide my actions and words that my attitude may be that of a servant as I follow Your leading. In Jesus' Name. Amen.

Points to ponder:

Who do you know that demonstrates a servant's heart? What sets them apart from others? Are you like them? How can you demonstrate a servant's heart today?

A Forever Friend

Topic of the day: friend

Definition: a person attached to another by feelings of affection or personal regard; a supporter

Words from the scriptures:

Revelation 3:15-22

Example of Jesus:

John 15:14-15

Daily meditation:

On a wall in my grandmother's house there hung the familiar picture of Jesus knocking at a door. As a child I assumed it was Jesus visiting a friend's house, like that of Mary and Martha and Lazarus. It was not until many years after my grandmother died when that picture hung in my house that I realized the picture represented the verses in Revelation. Jesus knocks at the doors of our lives seeking an invitation to enter so that we may be visited by the Dearest of Friends. There is no knob on the outside of that door. We must open it from the inside to allow admission by the Savior.

Prayer of my heart:

My Lord and my Savior, Thank You for coming into my heart and being my Dearest Friend forever. In Your wonderful Name. Amen.

Points to ponder:

Is Jesus still waiting for your invitation? Won't you ask Him in right now? Is He your Dearest Friend?

A Sleeping God

Topic of the day: voice

Definition: communication that comes through the mouth; figurative of God speaking to His people

Words from the scriptures:

Psalm 46:1-3, 10-11
1 Timothy 6:13-16
Joel 3:16

Example of Jesus:

John 10:1-5

Daily meditation:

Where is God when you need Him? Asleep? Hiding? Certainly not where you are. Then whose fault is that? God's? We'd love to blame God, or anyone else for that matter, for our own failures or falling away from God. Our less-than-wonderful responses to our spouses or children or friends must be someone else's doing. Certainly not ours. Our poor examples and witness to those who do not know the Lord can't be our faults.

Why then doesn't God answer us when we call? Perhaps because we aren't listening to His response or we don't want to hear what He really has to say to us. He invites us to draw near to Him (James 4:8). He's always there waiting. The move is ours. Too often we move farther away from God because of our own sin and worldliness, our own self-pity or conceit.

God calls us to be still and hear His voice (Psalm 46:10) but He speaks in small sounds and too often our ears are too deaf or too full of ourselves to hear Him speak.

Prayer of my heart:

I know You hear my prayer, oh Lord. Help me to move near to You that I may hear Your Voice speaking to me. Let nothing separate me from You. I pray in the Name of Jesus. Amen.

Points to ponder:

How much daily alone time do you have with the Lord? What is speaking to you if not the Lord? Have you stopped to listen for His still, small voice? Do you want to hear His voice and be led by Him? If so, what will you do about it?

Acceptance

Topic of the day: acceptance

Definition: to receive or approve with favor

Words from the scriptures:

Romans 15:7

Example of Jesus:

John 3:31-36

Daily meditation:

What would my day be like if I put others first? Would that make me a more worthy person? And worthy of what? Jesus accepts me as I am. He loves me and died for me just as I am.

Because I love Him, accept His sacrifice for me, I want to do what He has asked of me—to love others like He loves them. We are each His children, totally accepted by Him, no matter what we look like, feel like or act like. The difference is Him living in me and that makes all the difference, every day.

Prayer of my heart:

I praise You, Lord. Thank You, Lord. I want to put others before myself so I can exemplify Your love. Help me, Lord. In Jesus' Name. Amen.

Points to ponder:

What stops you from accepting yourself? What interferes with how you view others? Do you know that Jesus loves you right now, as you are? Do you accept His love? Do you want to share His love with others?

Acquisitions

Topic of the day: acquisitions

Definition: the act of gaining possession; something acquired

Words from the scriptures:

Matthew 6:31-34
Luke 12:17-20
Matthew 6:19-21

Example of Jesus:

Matthew 6:24-25

Daily meditation:

When we began packing to relocate after retiring, I was amazed to see how much "stuff" we had. Some of it I hadn't used or looked at in years. Why did I have it in the first place or keep it for so long?

As my son's family prepared to move they were surrounded by their "stuff." Should they keep it all? Even as the children surveyed their acquisitions they made lists of what they wanted for their upcoming birthdays. How could they need "more stuff?"

These episodes remind me of how I sometimes approach my prayers. God has provided for me abundantly, but I continue to want Him to give me more. Rather than acknowledge that all I have is His alone I continue to hoard "my" things.

When will I learn to surrender it all to Jesus to whom it belongs anyway? When will I think more of holding on to a growing relationship with my Savior than I do of my "precious worldly possessions?"

Prayer of my heart:

Lord, call my attention to the things of Your kingdom rather than my worldly mindset. Help me to seek You first and only hold on to what You consider important. In Jesus' Name I pray. Amen.

Points to ponder:

What is your most valued possession? What makes it most valued? Are you holding on to too much "stuff?" How can you "declutter" your life and concentrate on Christ? Won't you begin today?

Anxieties

Topic of the day: anxiety

Definition: uneasiness, fearfulness, worry

Words from the scriptures:

John 16:22-28
Philippians 4:6-7

Example of Jesus:

John 16:33b

Daily meditation:

Have you ever wondered why you concern yourself with some of the things that bother you? I have had some days begin with my hair out of place or a button missing from my blouse. These are trivial but they can be allowed to be consuming. Our Lord has promised us that He will meet our every need if we will ask Him (Matthew 7:7). He didn't qualify that by telling us He would only take care of the "big" deals in our lives. Our pride often keeps us from confiding in Him and allowing Him to solve those problems. We sacrifice the peace that God would have us enjoy when we allow ourselves to think we can handle things alone. When time passes and we are separated from *those* problems and other things have come up we wonder how the original issues could have troubled us at all. Giving it all to Jesus at the outset saves us from the turmoil and confusion of any anxiety. Surrender those concerns to Him right now.

Prayer of my heart:

Thank You, Almighty God, for helping me keep things in perspective. Help me to surrender any anxiety to You. Grant me the peace that only You can give. Amen.

Points to ponder:

What concerns you today? Are they the same things that concerned you yesterday? Why can't you turn your concerns over to the Lord? What do you expect the Lord to do for you?

Are You Still Sleeping?

Topic of the day: sleep

Definition: rest; mental dullness; laziness; figurative for death

Words from the scriptures:

Luke 22:45-46
1 Corinthians 15:34a

Example of Jesus:

Mark 13:35-37

Daily meditation:

Were the disciples physically or spiritually asleep while they were with Jesus at Gethsemane? Even though they had been His companions for three years and had observed His healing and feeding miracles, they still didn't understand His message of God's plan for salvation. Jesus had taught; they still expected something more.

What do I expect from Jesus? A plush job, easy money, wonderful relationships, great kids, smooth sailing, no problems? No suffering in this life? My attitude reveals that that is exactly what I expect. I am spiritually as asleep as the disciples were. I have the examples of all that Jesus did. I have the evidence in my own life of the miracles the Lord has performed for me and yet I still expect more. And if He doesn't deliver on my time schedule I begin to doubt His love for me and wander off to do my own thing. Then the words return, "I will never leave thee nor forsake thee (Joshua 1:5b KJV). Even while I am spiritually sleeping, God is at work in my life.

Prayer of my heart:

Heavenly Father, thank You for always being with me and forgiving my stubbornness. This I pray in the Name of Christ, my Lord. Amen.

Points to ponder:

How is God teaching you His lessons? Are you growing more aware of Christ daily? Do you see Him at work in your life? If not, why not? Maybe it's time for you to wake up to what God is trying to say to you. Start right now.

Weeds and Waterspots

Topic of the day: weeds

Definition: valueless plant growing wild, especially one that grows on cultivated ground to the exclusion or injury of the desired crop; any undesirable or troublesome plant, especially one that grows profusely where it is not wanted

Words from the scriptures:

1 John 1:9

Example of Jesus:

Matthew 13:23-25

Daily meditation:

When I moved to the country I didn't realize that the almost constant blowing of the wind would bring weed seeds to my yard. If I immediately pulled the growing weeds out of the flower beds I could maintain them, but if I put off the dreaded job of weed pulling the chore became much more difficult. Nor did I know that the water in my well was so hard that every surface it touched would have water stains if the water was not immediately wiped off.

Sin in our lives can be very much like the weeds in the yard or the water spots on the counters. It blows in constantly and can be felt in every area of our being. Sometimes we notice it right away and confess it and the Lord mercifully forgives us. We've pulled out the weeds or wiped off the water. At other times we ignore our sin or procrastinate taking it to the Lord for confession until it has overgrown our life like the weeds I didn't pull immediately or covered us like the water stains that were not wiped off quickly. The sin requires much more effort to eliminate. That doesn't mean that the sin can't be done away with, but the task may become more difficult.

The Lord is faithful to forgive our sins whenever we confess them, but we must first confess them to Him. How much more joy for our lives if we handle sin quickly when we first become aware of it. That way the sin doesn't become a weed in our flower bed that can take over and choke out the flowers or a stain on the relationship that we want to have with our Savior.

Prayer of my heart

Lord of my life, I want the Holy Spirit to show me all the areas I need to confess to You that I may be cleansed and renewed in my walk with You. Thank You for Your willingness to free me from the sins I commit. In Jesus' Name. Amen.

Points to ponder:

Is there sin in your life that keeps you from that close walk you desire with Jesus? Why not bring it to the throne of grace right now and be cleansed?

Where Is Your Faith?

Topic of the day: faith

Definition: reliance, loyalty, or complete trust in God or someone else

Words from the scriptures:

Matthew 6: 26-34

Example of Jesus:

Matthew 15:28a
Matthew 21:21
Matthew 15:31b

Daily meditation:

Have you ever considered that every time you sit down on a chair you are trusting the manufacturer to have built the chair properly, that it will hold you, and you will not fall on the floor? Or that when you drive down the road in your car the other drivers will stay on their side of the road? Yet we do this and much more in our daily routines. But in our spiritual lives we want God to prove Himself over and over before we will take that simple step of faith, putting our trust in Him for everything in our lives. He is our Provider and He cares for us and will meet our every need.

Once when I was very upset and depressed and shared that with my dad, his response to me was, "Where is your faith? Don't you know God doesn't give up?" Where is your faith today? Do you trust in the Lord to handle every circumstance?

Prayer of my heart:

Dear Lord, forgive me for testing You. Help me to trust You daily for all I have need of. Thank You for providing for me. Amen.

Points to ponder:

In what do you put your trust? Which of life's circumstances do you need to hand over to the Lord today?

Who Is My Neighbor?

Topic of the day: neighbor

Definition: member of one's community

Words from the scriptures:

Matthew 19:16, 21-22
Luke 10:24-37

Example of Jesus:

Matthew 10:32-42

Daily meditation:

"Who is my neighbor?" was a question asked of Jesus. The one who asked the question didn't like the answer Jesus gave him. What questions do I ask the Lord then turn my back on His response?

The word tells us to meet the needs of others, love our enemies, visit the sick, and minister to the widows and orphans. All too often we respond with, "but you don't mean me, Lord. There must be someone else."

In this global age of instant communication our neighborhood has grown. We know of the needs around the world in a matter of seconds. Organizations sometimes come when called, like the Red Cross or other humanitarian groups, for disaster relief. Military assistance is sometimes sent to aid alliances.

But what are we doing to fulfill the Great Commission (Matthew 28:19-20) in our neighborhoods. It is not the responsibility of missionaries and doctors alone. It is not the obligation of the government of any country. Our neighbors are calling to us. How are we following Christ's example in meeting their needs?

It really comes down to whom I will serve: myself or my Lord and Master.

Prayer of my heart

Lord, thank You for examples of how to share. Thank You for Your Holy Spirit to lead and guide us in our humble efforts. Show us which neighbor needs us now that Your Good News will fill the world. In Jesus' Name and for His sake I lift this prayer. Amen.

Points to ponder:

Who are you serving today? Which neighbor's need will you meet today? How is your relationship with your neighbors? What needs to change? What will you do to change it? When will you start?

Waiting

Topic of the day: waiting

Definition: patiently anticipating

Words from the scriptures:

Psalm 40:1
Isaiah 30:18

Example of Jesus:

Luke 12:35-37

Daily meditation:

Consider what you wait for in any given day. Stop lights, pedestrians, checking out at the grocery store, the mail. In a specific year you may wait for a wedding day, the birth of a baby, or a visit from a friend or relative. Many of our waited-for events are trivial, but some have great significance for us but waiting is required.

Some things we wait for patiently, some not so patiently. Some things we may even be reluctant to receive like news from a physician about a health condition or the cost of repairs on our cars or homes. But wait we do.

Do we wait in prayer for a message from the Master? Do we await His daily presence? How do we wait for the Lord? Are we patiently preparing for His return or have we forgotten He's coming? Are we ready to meet the Lord on His return? Are we expectant or in dread? Are we going about His business in His absence or only dealing with our own? How we wait for Jesus says a lot about our relationship to Him. Do we wait for Him right now?

Prayer of my heart:

Savior, may I wait expectantly daily for Your return and do what You want done while I anticipate You. In Christ's blessed Name, I pray. Amen.

Points to ponder:

Is Jesus your personal Savior? How do you demonstrate that relationship in the things you wait for? What would you do differently today if you knew Jesus would come tomorrow?

The Little Things

Topic of the day: action

Definition: the process of doing

Words from the scriptures:

Ephesians 4:32
Romans 12:1-3
Hebrews 10:19-25

Example of Jesus:

Matthew 7:9-12

Daily meditation:

Frantically searching for the other shoe, gathering books, lunch money, and children, I furtively glanced at the clock. Yes, we'd be late again. It wasn't any one thing that caused the daily melee. We got up in plenty of time. It was our failure to adequately plan for all the little things in the routine that upset what would have been everything on schedule.

As I reflected on this, I realized my Christian walk is often this way. I run around to meetings at church. I prepare to teach Sunday school or practice the anthem for choir. But I am late for my own spiritual renewal because I cut short my quiet time or Bible reading. I fail to attend to the "little things" that provide real life for my spiritual growth and development. How can we keep the Lord's word at the forefront of our daily activities?

Prayer of my heart:

Dear Lord, thank You for reminding me that I depend on You alone for my life. Help me to handle the vital "little things" as You direct. In my Savior's Name I pray today. Amen.

Points to ponder:

What interrupts your time alone with the Lord? How can you change that? What is the first step?

Jesus Faced Temptation

Was it like mine?

Topic of the day: temptation

Definition: to entice someone to sin; cause of enticement

Words from the scriptures:

Matthew 26:41
1 Corinthians 10:13
Hebrews 2:18

Example of Jesus:

Luke 4:1-2
Matthew 4:1-11
Mark 1:12-13

Daily meditation:

In the scriptures Jesus has given us many examples of how we are to live our lives. Our problem is we don't always read the scriptures and when we do we don't meditate or memorize them. When Jesus faced temptations from the Pharisees and others who wanted to undermine His message, including the face-to-face confrontation with the devil in the wilderness, Jesus met the opposition with scriptures. It was committed to memory. He knew the way to put the devil to flight no matter what form he took.

How often do I face the challenges of life unprepared? I have not put on the full armor of God (Ephesians 6:10-17) and do not know the Word. James tells us to "resist the devil and he will flee from you." (James 4:7 NKJV) Our resistance to the influence of Satan comes from knowing the Word of God. How prepared are you to meet temptations today?

Prayer of my heart:

Holy God, thank You for Your Word. Help me to learn it so I am prepared for the attacks from the evil one. Help me to resist the temptations of this world, no matter what form they take. In Jesus' Name I commit this prayer. Amen.

Points to ponder:

What was the greatest temptation you ever faced? How did you handle it? What will you do the next time you are tempted? How will you prepare yourself to face temptations?

Take Each Day

Topic of the day: burdens

Definition: to disturb mentally or physically; afflict, distress

Words from the scriptures:

Psalm 142:1-7
II Corinthians 4:16

Example of Jesus:

John 16:22-24

Daily meditation:

I had reached the end of my fragile balance between handling daily pressures and feeling totally out of control. I was out of control on all fronts. Tears streamed down my face and I felt like God had deserted me. After all He'd promised if we asked in faith, He would grant our petitions and I had not just asked but begged for things to get better in my life. Yet here I was.

It was then, in my desperation, that I could see clearly my dependence on Him. On my heavenly Father only. Nothing else could make things better. I certainly couldn't do anything more. The whole burden had to be given to the Lord. Once I gave it all unconditionally to Him, He could handle it on my behalf. But as long as I tried to keep some things under my thumb God's work and His glory could not be seen. He couldn't "make things better."

Today wasn't perfect. It wasn't even good, but it was better and I can see the Lord anew at work in my life.

Prayer of my heart:

Thank You, Father, for helping me always in every circumstance of my life. Amen.

Points to ponder:

What troubles you today? What can you do to change things? What do you expect God to do? Have you turned things over to Him? Why don't you do it now?

Submission

Topic of the day: submission

Definition: voluntarily yield to the power of another

Words from the scriptures:

Isaiah 55:8-11
Proverbs 22:6
Hebrews 12:9

Example of Jesus:

John 14:6

Daily meditation:

The yelling started when I would not allow my son to do something he felt he ought to be permitted to do. I refused to yield and ended the conversation. Later I overheard him reply to a friend, "No, I can't tonight; maybe some other time." No hostility or anger, just fact. I was overjoyed at his submission to the rules.

The parallel I saw to my own life was humbling. How often I rebel against my Father's will for me and I yell. I create havoc and confusion for myself in my "fit." Peace only comes when I submit my will to the Father's and stop insisting on my own way. His plan for me is so much safer for me than my plan for myself.

Jesus calls us to be submissive to Him in all things. How are you doing?

Prayer of my heart:

Heavenly Father, thank You for not letting go of me no matter how I rebel. Thank You for my child's lesson to me. Help me to submit my will to Yours in all things. In Christ's name I pray. Amen.

Points to ponder:

Have you ever rebelled against God? What was the result? What did you learn from the experience? Are you submissive to God?

Spheres of Influence

Topic of the day: influence

Definition: the capacity or power of persons or things to be a compelling force on or produce effects on actions, behavior, opinions, etc., of others

Words from the scriptures:

1 Chronicles 4:10
Isaiah 55:11

Example of Jesus:

Matthew 28:19-20

Daily meditation:

We have no idea what impact we will have on the lives of others. We sometimes try to persuade others to think like we do. Sometimes we are asked for an opinion or advice on some issue. We have responsibilities to our families and friends, to organizations and our churches. This provides a certain amount of potential influence in each of those circles. But we seldom know the results of our words and actions in these activities. Therefore we should be cautious of how we behave and what we say because we never know who is watching or what the outcome will be.

Are we seeking to widen our contacts, to broaden our spheres of influence? Do we care enough to pray like Jabez that we might influence more for Christ's sake?

Prayer of my heart:

May I be ready to be used by You as you use the impact of my life for Your glory, oh God. In Jesus' Name. Amen.

Points to ponder:

Who do you influence? Who else would you like to influence? What can you do to accomplish that?

Smiles

Topic of the day: smile

Definition: to assume a facial expression indicating pleasure or favor

Words from the scriptures:

Numbers 6:24-26
Proverbs 15:13

Example of Jesus:

Matthew 5:46-48

Daily meditation:

Today my heart was made glad when someone smiled at me. It was not someone I know only a person I passed on my way to the grocery store. Another person said "hello" in a very pleasant way. I was surprised by the warmth in the chillness of the wind and responded "good morning."

I decided to make today a pleasure to someone else by passing on a gracious smile or a warm hello because it does make a difference if we acknowledge others, even those we do not know. As Christians we are to reflect the image of Christ. What are others seeing or hearing as they pass us on the street? How much nicer would our world become if we shared the Lord's love in word and deed with everyone we meet. It can be a simple smile or just hello.

Prayer of my heart:

Lord Jesus, let me reflect Your image to all I meet today. Amen.

Points to ponder:

What has made you glad recently? What greeting can you share with those you meet today?

Who Is Our Guide?

Topic of the day: guide

Definition: one who gives direction

Words from the scriptures:

Psalm 7:1
Psalm 50:1-15
1 Peter 5:6-7

Example of Jesus:

John 16:12-15

Daily meditation:

It was nearly dusk as I drove through a blinding rain storm en route to my sister's. Even as the windshield wipers flew back and forth my eyes were drawn to a break in the clouds where a patch of blue sky was surrounded by white puffy clouds in the midst of the gray-black turbulence.

How like life that storm seemed to me. Moments of peace surrounded by turmoil if we do not keep our eyes properly focused on the One who is our Guide on the roadway of life. But what a comfort for each day is the signpost of the cross and the perfect love it demonstrated.

Prayer of my heart:

Heavenly Father, thank You for being my Guide for every step of my life. Help me to continue in Your way. In Jesus' Name. Amen.

Points to ponder:

Where is your focus today? Are the troubles of life and the cares of the world engulfing you? What would it feel like if you "cast your burdens on Him?" What keeps you from that surrender to the Lord? Why not give it all to Him right now?

What Does A Miracle Look Like

Topic of the day: miracles

Definition: an effect or extraordinary event in the physical world that surpasses all known human or natural powers and is ascribed to a supernatural cause; such an effect or event manifesting or considered as a work of God

Words from the scriptures:

Psalm 77:14

Example of Jesus:

Luke 7:22

Daily meditation:

What does a miracle look like?

A new job or financial success,
Lunch with a friend,
Saving a kitten from a tree,
A sunrise or sunset,
Lightning cutting through storm clouds,
A budding rose or tree in bloom,

A new born baby,
The love of family,
The healing of an illness or broken heart,
The love of God that brings salvation, rescuing a sinner from hell?

These are all miracles to me.

Prayer of my heart:

Dear God of all the miracles around me, thank You for Your continuing presence in my life and this world. Help me to see Your hand at work daily in the miracles You show me. Amen.

Points to ponder:

What miracles are in your life? Do you thank God for them daily? Do you recognize His work around you or are you focusing on yourself? Right now thank Him for His miracles in your life.

Wake Up and Repent

Topic of the day: repentance

Definition: deep sorrow, compunction, or contrition for a past sin, wrong doing; regret for any past action.

Words from the scriptures:

Joel 1:2
Psalm 51:12
Revelation 3:1-3
1 John 1:9

Example of Jesus:

Mark 1:3-5

Daily meditation:

Wake Up

Wake up, see your sin
Stop making excuses
God knows anyway
The mess that you are in.

Wake up, confess your faults
Accept the forgiveness
Jesus offered by His sacrifice
On Calvary's cross.

Wake up, repent, and retrieve
The life God will give you when you
Go forward in the love
The Savior wants to be yours.

Prayer of my heart:

Gracious Lord, my Savior. I pray that Your people will wake up and take a stand for Truth and that those who do not know You will accept Your saving grace now. This I pray in the Name of Jesus. Amen.

Points to ponder:

What keeps you from turning from things you know are wrong? What keeps you from accepting the forgiveness Christ offers? Won't you turn to Him right now?

Visiting the Sick

Topic of the day: sick

Definition: ill, in bad health

Words from the scriptures:

Matthew 25:34-45
James 4:2b

Example of Jesus:

Matthew 7:7-8

Daily meditation:

One day I had a conversation with a woman I met at church. She was dissatisfied with a church she'd been attending because when her children were ill for an extended time no one even called to ask what the matter was. I queried whether she had made her need known to those in the church. She thought they should have realized on their own. Perhaps the absences should have been noticed and calls made. Christ has told us in His Word to visit the sick; He has also told us we should let others know of our needs. Other people cannot read our minds.

In my own life I harbored resentment and pain like this woman because I failed to tell people what I expected and needed from them. Once I shared my needs with my Christian brothers and sisters I was blessed on every side with the generosity of Christ through their love and sharing.

How much of our pain and suffering is self-inflicted? How much peace are we denied because of our self-centeredness? It's time to share so we can be ministered to as well as minister to others.

Prayer of my heart:

Heavenly Father, thank You for the love of fellow Christians. Help us to meet each other's needs as they are made known to us. In Jesus' Name. Amen.

Points to ponder:

Who do you need to reach out to in order to minister to them? What do you need to share with others so they can minister to you?

The Lord's Message

Topic of the day: witness

Definition: to see, hear, or know by personal presence and perception; to be present at (an occurrence) as a formal witness, spectator, bystander; to bear witness to, testify to, give or afford evidence of

Words from the scriptures:

1 Thessalonians 1:8-10

Example of Jesus:

Acts 1:8

Daily meditation:

The Old Testament gives us testimony of who Jesus is and what He will do on earth as well as in the lives of people. The New Testament gives us the life of Christ and His ministry while He was physically with people on earth. Our lives as believers should give expression to who Christ is in our individual lives as we share the Good News with others. The Bible is written information for our use as we grow in our relationship with Christ. But our lives are "the only Bible some people ever read." How are we sharing Christ as we go through our daily chores, jobs, experiences? Do people see a loving, caring Jesus in me or will they reject Jesus because of me?

Prayer of my heart:

My Savior, let my life reflect Your love so others may come to know you as I know You. Never let me be the cause for others to reject Your sacrifice for sins. In Your loving Name I pray. Amen.

Points to ponder:

What does my daily routine of activities say about my Jesus, my relationship with Him, and my love for others? Do I need to change anything? Am I allowing Jesus and His Holy Spirit to lead me?

The Blood of the Lamb

Topic of the day: blood

Definition: fluid in circulatory system; signifies human life; of animals, used in sacrifices; of Christ, effective for the forgiveness of sins; on hands or head, symbolic of guilt

Words from the scriptures:

Exodus 24:8
Romans 3:21-22
Romans 5:9
1 Corinthians 11:25

Example of Jesus:

Matthew 26:26-28

Daily meditation:

In the spring we shear our sheep. Our sheep are the very white variety called Dorset. In the process of shearing the sheep nicks occur and blood spews forth. One ewe had blood all down her head, covering her face. I wondered if a main blood vessel had been hit in the process of shearing her wool. The stark contrast of her white body and the bloody red of her head reminded me of the blood shed by

Jesus on the cross that covers my sin. The difference between Christ's perfect Life and my imperfect one was portrayed by that shearing accident. The ewe survived and so do I because of Calvary and the sacrifice of my Savior there for me.

Prayer of my heart:

Dear Lord Jesus, thank You for dying for me that I might live forever with You. Amen.

Points to ponder:

Have you submitted your life to Jesus and allowed His blood to cover your sins as you confess them before Him? If you have not do that right now. If you have become a Christ follower are you sharing His saving grace offered freely to you with others? If not, why not?

Stunted Growth

Topic of the day: grow

Definition: to increase by natural development

Words from the scriptures:

Job 8:11-12
Psalm 104:13-15
Jonah 4:5-7

Example of Jesus:

Matthew 13:24-30

Daily meditation:

The soil in my garden is not the best for growing my vegetables. It is too alkaline. The things I try to grow often appear too small to be of any value in our food cellar. However, with proper soil aids and fertilizer I can enhance the crop's growth and make production higher.

I am reminded of my need for spiritual growth. My spiritual growth can be stunted if the soil is improperly prepared. I can become so self-absorbed that I produce no fruit. My growth is stunted.

The Lord wants to provide me the nutrients I require for proper growth, but if I am not available for reading His Word or hearing His voice my production will be worthless like that of my improperly prepared garden. I must turn my attention to the leading of the Holy Spirit to grow the way God intended for me to develop and not have my growth stunted. Only in that way can I become the person God wants me to be.

Prayer of my heart:

Creator of all things, thank You for providing food for our spiritual growth. May my growth never be stunted because I stop feeding on Your Word and submitting to Your leading. In Jesus' Name. Amen.

Points to ponder:

What kind of soil are you preparing? Has your spiritual growth become stunted? What "treatments" can you provide to restart the growth process?

Spectator Seats

/

Topic of the day: spectators

Definition: a person who looks on, observes, onlooker; member of an audience

Words from the scriptures:

Revelation 2:2-7
Luke 23:48-49

Example of Jesus:

Luke 2:46-52

Daily meditation:

Jesus chose to be in the thick of things. As a school teacher it is interesting to observe those who arrive on the first day of school and take seats in the front row of the classroom. There are two groups of students who do this. Those who arrive last and who are forced by circumstances to sit there because there are no other seats left in the classroom and those who opt for a front row seat so that they can be active participants in the action that takes place within the class. Equally fascinating is the third group of students who are those who select the back row. I observe them to be the non-participants, the spectators.

How like our Christian walk these groups are. There are those of us who sit up front, who participate in the Lord's work on earth and are about His business by overt choices we make. There are those of us forced to take action by circumstances that the Lord provides for us. Then there is the third group. There are those of us who are observers in the spectator seats of Christ's work.

Which group describes your work for the Lord?

Prayer of my heart:

Lord, help me to take the place that You have designed for me and not to mistakenly be a spectator of the Kingdom's work on earth. In Christ's Holy Name. Amen.

Points to ponder:

What kind of worker are you? Do you volunteer to do things or wait to be asked to do something? Are you available and willing to work on things that will glorify the Lord or do you hesitate to get involved? Are you a spectator or are you an involved participant?

Savior

Topic of the day: Savior

Definition: one who delivers from trouble, sin, or judgment

Words from the scriptures:

Isaiah 43:11
Isaiah 60:16b
Isaiah 62:11
1 Timothy 4:10

Example of Jesus:

John 4:10-14, 25-26

Daily meditation:

What is in your savings account? Are you saving for a future vacation, summer home or retirement? Too often we rely on the things of this earth to meet our perceived needs. We may not be thinking about an eternal future. The Bible shows us many examples of people who looked to the coming of a Savior. They knew there was more to come than what they were currently experiencing. Many relied on provision from God. They trusted Him to satisfy their every need.

We have many excuses for not accepting the Messiah today. Sometimes we have obligations that keep us so busy each day we don't even think about Jesus. But as we look at the world around us and the increasing chaos that is occurring, the growing evil activities, the unending hardships, it's time to get right with God. There may not be tomorrow. Procrastination no longer has a place in our lives. We must meet Jesus now and live for Him daily. No other purpose makes any sense in the eternal scheme of things. How is your eternal savings account growing?

Prayer of my heart:

Jesus, Messiah, Savior, thank You for providing a home in heaven for me. Help me live each day to further Your Kingdom. I lift high the Name of Jesus, my Savior. Amen.

Points to ponder:

What are you relying on to save you from eternal damnation? Do you know the Lord, Jesus Christ as your Savior? If you don't, why not ask Him into your heart right now?

Remember Whose You Are

Topic of the day: belonging

Definition: to be in the relation of a member, adherent, inhabitant

Words from the scriptures:

Romans: 8:31-37

Example of Jesus:

Mark 9:40-42
John 17:9-12, 24-26
John 16:33

Daily meditation:

When my children were young, whenever they would leave to where I wasn't going, I would tell them to," Remember whose you are." At first glance the phrase seemed to mean: "remember who your mother is and don't embarrass me." Instead between us the phrase meant something different. It meant they belonged to Jesus and He would go before them and beside them in every circumstance they faced. He would protect them even if I couldn't.

I don't know if it helped my children during those growing up years or not. But the phrase reminds me today that I belong to Jesus and no matter what issues I deal with or problems I encounter He will protect me from the evil one if I simply call on Him.

Do you know the love and peace Jesus provides? Ask Him to meet your needs right now.

Prayer of my heart:

Jesus, Jesus, Jesus. Even Your name protects me. Thank You for all You are doing for me today because I belong to You. In that sweet, sweet Name, I pray. Amen.

Points to ponder:

What belongs to you? To whom or what do you belong? Do you belong to Jesus? If not, why not accept Him right now and belong to Him for eternity?

Religion vs. Relationship

Topic of the day: relationship

Definition: a connection, association, involvement; an emotional connection between people

Words from the scriptures:

Psalm 24:4-6
Romans 1:16-17
Romans 5:17-19

Example of Jesus:

Luke 12:21-22

Daily meditation:

Jesus has called us to follow certain rules of conduct as Christians. Our desire to serve Jesus makes us want to behave like He did. We do not need a check list of things we must do to be followers of Christ. Instead we are led by the Holy Spirit into a walk with Messiah, Who gave us the example of how to behave. We have His Word as a Guidebook for our path in this life.

We sacrifice the peace Jesus promised when we attempt to live our daily lives in the power of our own strength rather than calling upon the Holy Spirit to prepare our ways. An old hymn says it well, "O, what peace we often forfeit; o what needless pain we bear, All because we do not carry everything to God in prayer." ("What a Friend We Have in Jesus," Joseph Scriven, 1855.)

The relationship we have with Christ is not a set of rules we are compelled to follow or dogma dictated by a church. It is a heart-felt longing to walk in the footsteps Jesus sets before us so we can draw closer to Him with every step.

Prayer of my heart:

Jesus, thank You for Your example for living here on earth. May my relationship with You deepen daily and not be encumbered by a to-do-list that You did not intend to be a part of my life. Guide every step of all my days. In the Name of Jesus. Amen.

Points to ponder:

What is your religion? Do you have a relationship with the Savior or are you practicing a "religion?" Are you growing in a personal relationship with Christ or checking off requirements imposed by a church? What is hindering your progress in your relationship with Jesus? Won't you invite Jesus to be your Guide right now?

Rehearsal for the Big Event

Topic of the day: rehearse

Definition: to practice in private prior to a public presentation; to drill or train

Words from the scriptures:

Psalm 106:1-5
Galatians 5:18-24
Revelation 22:10-12

Example of Jesus:

John 3:20-21

Daily meditation:

When I was a member of our church adult choir we put on a Christmas musical. This was a major undertaking in our church, complete with a "living tree" that the choir would stand in to sing. The choir began practicing the music at a "Christmas in September" kickoff event. Children learned the words and motions for their heralding the arrival of the Baby Jesus. Volunteers would take the tree parts out of storage and "build" it in late November in preparation for the big event.

Rehearsals were held on Saturdays in November so everyone could identify where they would stand in the tree and how they would climb up the steps and pop up in their places. There had to be enough room for all the singers in the tree and the stage in front of it had to be large enough to hold the children's choirs and soloists. Music was memorized and a final dress rehearsal was held a few days before the opening production.

This was an example to me of how we should be preparing for Jesus' return and our meeting of Him. Daily we should be rehearsing His message with others and our actions should reflect the anticipation we have of seeing Jesus face to face. This should not be a rehearsal for a Christmas production, important as that is in sharing the Gospel, but a preparation for the Big Event—eternity with our Savior.

Prayer of my heart:

Lord, may my days be rehearsals that prepare me for my life with You. May my words and actions speak only, always, of my love for You. In Your Name, I pray. Amen.

Points to ponder:

What events in your life have you prepared for? Do you prepare to meet Jesus face to face? How do you do that? What else might you do or what would you change if you were committed to that preparation daily?

Christmas Is Over

Topic of the day: Christ

Definition: Jesus of Nazareth, the fulfillment of prophecies in the Old Testament regarding the eventual coming of a Messiah; the Messiah prophesied in the Old Testament (used chiefly in versions of the New Testament).

Words from the scriptures:

Isaiah 9:6-7 (New International Version)

Example of Jesus:

Matthew 16:13-17

Daily meditation:

Christmas is over. Baby Jesus is gone. Or is He? The tree is bare; the decorations stowed away. The manger is wrapped and stored for the year along with the Baby Jesus figure. But is the Jesus we know just the figure in the manger scene at Christmastime? The Christ of Christmas is alive and living in our hearts and lives as we share His message of love in our daily activities throughout the year. When we call a lonely shut-in to say hello or take food to a grieving family in their time of loss. When we smile at a harried mother shopping in the grocery store or offer to care for a sick person or serve food at a soup kitchen. Even when we least realize it our actions speak loudly of our love of the Messiah who came at Christmas.

The holiday celebration may be behind us for another year, but the joy of the message of the Savior will go out all through the new year. We are never separated from the Christ Who came that Christmas day and as His followers we share His letter of love every day.

Prayer of my heart:

Jesus, Messiah, Savior, may my life reflect Your love for us each and every day as I go about my routine activities. Thank You for never being far from me. Amen.

Points to ponder:

Who do you think Jesus is? Do you know Him as the Messiah, Savior of your life? If not, why not accept Him right now?

Prisoner of Circumstances

Topic of the day: circumstances

Definition: a condition, detail, part, or attribute, with respect to time, place, manner, agent, etc., that accompanies, determines, or modifies a fact or event; a modifying or influencing factor

Words from the scriptures:

Jeremiah 29:13
2 Corinthians 4:6-18

Example of Jesus:

John 8:31-32
John 14:27

Daily meditation:

In the solitude, an often sought after commodity seldom found, I felt as if my heart would break. There have been times in my life of utter sadness, but there were reasons for that: my grandmother died; I was jilted by a love; I went away to college. Those were painful times. But today, this heartache had no identifiable source. Only a multitude of life's burdens built up and smashed down. Things out of control and overwhelming: economic problems, disobedient children, unloving thoughts. I recognized my need to submit my total will to the Master's plan.

I had to change because the only thing I could change was me. God alone knew how this would be resolved. This vague grief over circumstances I could not change, but the pain I felt was real. God can heal the heart and provide comfort in the midst of tears. In fact, only God can accomplish this. And He will only succeed if we are submitted to Him in our whole heart. Only then can we be free in deed. (John 8:32)

Prayer of my heart:

Lord, thank You for the freedom You have given me and that You offer to others. In Jesus' Name I pray. Amen.

Points to ponder:

Do you feel overwhelmed by circumstances that are beyond your control? Why not give them to the Lord right now so He can bring you peace?

Prejudice: A Stumbling Block

Topic of the day: prejudice

Definition: an unfavorable opinion or feeling formed beforehand or without knowledge, thought, or reason

Words from the scriptures:

Romans 14:10-13
Romans 14:19
Romans 15:4

Example of Jesus:

John 15:13

Daily meditation:

I was a high school teacher for many years. More than once in my career when students appeared for the opening of school I singled out one who looked like he or she didn't belong there with the rest of the students: hair too long, pants too baggy, too many piercings or tattoos. The student's attitude was not appropriate and too often neither was the language or attire. You've seen the type. Sadly rather than looking for ways to help this student feel welcome or a part of the class we may have shunned this individual or added to the feeling of being unwanted or unaccepted he or she already felt.

Our Lord always looked beyond the appearance to meet the needs of the heart and soul. Paul admonishes us not to present interferences between our brothers and their seeking to do the Lord's will. In the cases where I have prejudged others, has my attitude prevented them from coming to the know the Savior? Have I failed to share God's love because I let my attitude and prejudice get in the way? Have I been a stumbling block to others? Forgive me, Lord. How is your attitude?

Prayer of my heart: Dear Lord, forgive my arrogant attitude in some dealings with those You love. Change the prejudice that gets in the way of my witness in the world. Help me to be an encourager not a discourager. I pray in Christ's Name. Amen.

Points to ponder:

Describe a prejudice you have. Is it God-honoring? If it is not, what can you do about it?

Our Light

Topic of the day: light

Definition: daytime brightness, illumination, exposure to truth

Words from the scriptures:

John 1:1-9

Example of Jesus:

John 8:12

Daily meditation:

For several weeks the light in my microwave oven had not come on as it should have. I got used to the inconvenience and assumed it was a burned out bulb. It wasn't worth the effort to try to fix it. Then I spent a week involved in events that turned out less than what I had hoped they would be and definitely not what I had prayed they would be like. As I reflected on this and just as I reached what felt like the bottom, I prayed again, "God, what do you want me to do?"

As I was praying I was also using the malfunctioning microwave oven. As I pulled out the heated plate "something" made the light come back on. It wasn't really burned out. It dawned on me as that light came on that all the Father wants me to do is trust Him at His Word to Light my path (Psalm 119:105) and to remember that no matter how dark the circumstances of my life "He will not leave me nor forsake me." (Psalm 27:9)

Prayer of my heart:

Lord, remind me that You are the Light of the world and want to Light my way wherever I go and in whatever I do. In Jesus' Name. Amen.

Points to ponder:

How can we light the world if we don't know the Light? How has Jesus lighted your day? Have you shared the Light with others?

Burden

Topic of the day: burden

Definition: that which is borne, physically or spiritually

Words from the scriptures:

Psalm 38:4
Psalm 68:19-20

Example of Jesus:

Luke 11:46
Matthew 11:28-30

Daily meditation:

Watching a child struggle to carry a heavy load causes most adults to want to assist the child. Observing an elderly person make their way cautiously across an intersection or to their car stimulates a similar response. It is not as natural a response to offer aid to someone near our own age or a haughty teenager. Sometimes the burdens they carry are not physically observable.

Nonetheless the emotional or spiritual burdens carried can be more debilitating that the physical ones. But since they are not as obvious we must pay attention to the things not said or the body language especially of those we know: family members, close friends, fellow Christians.

It is our responsibility to give our own personal loads to the Lord so we can be free of those burdens. We were never called to carry them. It is also our privilege to help others cast off their cares as we model, counsel, and confide in those around us. Lighten those loads today and see what a freedom you experience in Christ. Praise God! He has promised to make the burden "easy to be borne." (Matthew 11:30b AMPC)

Prayer of my heart:

Gracious Lord, thank You for sharing my burdens and refreshing my life daily. Help me to give You the problems of my life that I may be free to live in You. In Jesus' saving Name. Amen.

Points to ponder:

What needless burdens do you carry today? Who can you help find that freedom from the loads of care? What will be your first step today?

Clouds

Topic of the day: clouds

Definition: a visible collection of particles of water or ice suspended in the air, usually at an elevation about the earth's surface

Words from the scriptures:

Job 35:5

Example of Jesus:

Matthew 26:64

Daily meditation:

As I gazed at the clouds today I noticed they were moving rapidly across the sky. Some blue sky was visible among the clouds while some of the clouds touched the distant mountains. The patterns the clouds created kept changing, sometimes large clumps of clouds together, sometimes small clusters widely spread apart. Some even looked like you could reach out and touch them. In many ways this symbolizes our lives. It moves by quickly from day to day but never stays the same. No matter how much we want things to continue in the good times they don't and we move on. Other days we can't wait for things to change because of what is going on and the unpleasantness we are experiencing we want to end. It seems some times in our lives are clumps of problems, disasters or unbearable circumstances. Sometimes we can see the Lord up close and very near and other times He seems to be off in the distance. No matter which view we have He is always there to guide us. No matter how much our lives toss and turn us, He is ever-present to up lift us and comfort us. No matter how much things change God is the same forever.

Prayer of my heart:

Almighty God, Maker of heaven and earth, thank You for Your creation for me, for my life and for Your presence in my life. Amen.

Points to ponder:

What clouds seem to be covering God's presence in your life today? What are you doing to uncover Him right now?

Memorial Day

Topic of the day: memories

Definition: mental capacity or faculty of retaining and reviving facts, events, impressions etc., or of recalling or recognizing previous experiences

Words from the scriptures:

Psalm 145:6-8

Example of Jesus:

Matthew 26:12-13

Daily meditation:

Decoration Day was a celebration of those who died in the Civil War. Today on the Memorial Day holiday we honor all our dead, all who've passed on before us, some in war, some just passed from this life into eternity. But this is a day to remember them, to honor them. We mark the memory with flowers on graves, headstones, and inscriptions.

Other memories we create in our lives are captured in pictures, or with phrases like "sweet 16" or other special dates. We celebrate memorable events such as marriages, anniversaries, birthdays, or favorite times shared together at football games or proms. Many things in our lives become memories, some treasures, and some troubles.

I wonder what memories we have marked with the Savior. Are we making each day a memory with Jesus? What marks the memories? Have we moved on to grow closer to Jesus, to a more mature walk in faith or have we become lukewarm in our relationship to Christ? Jesus is the only Way to create memories that will last for eternity. Let His glory shine in the memories you make today. Make this a Memorial Day with Jesus.

Prayer of my heart:

My prayer for today is that Your memories of me will bring pleasantness to Your heart, dear Jesus. Amen.

Points to ponder:

Do memories shackle us or free us? Do we live in the past or go forward in Jesus' name?

Magnificent Might

Topic of the day: force

Definition: strength, energy, power, intensity

Words from the scriptures:

Psalm 89:9
Isaiah 30:30

Example of Jesus:

Mark 4:39

Daily meditation:

In the midst of a tornado or hurricane we probably wouldn't wonder at the power of God. As the rivers flood their banks and sweep away all in their paths we wouldn't deny God is in control. When volcanoes erupt and lava spews forth, there's no denying a greater force than man is at work. As flower buds colorfully unfurl and trees leaf to green, as soft rain falls on dried out dirt, God is magnified.

If God has orchestrated all the forces of nature to function and harmonize, and He has, why am I so reluctant to acknowledge His control in my life? I can't stop the strength of the wind nor calm the seas any more than I can stem the tides of my life. But God can. His mighty Hand is in charge of it all, always.

Prayer of my heart:

Heavenly Father, help me to surrender myself completely to Your will that every part of my life may be under Your control. Help me when I struggle even as You help me when I don't. May my life demonstrate Your control in all things. Thank you, Lord. Amen.

Points to ponder:

What is the greatest force of nature? Who controls it? What is the greatest challenge in your life today? Who controls that?

Lesson from a Child

Topic of the day: child

Definition: young person between infancy and youth; offspring or descendants

Words from the scriptures:

Psalm 138:8
Proverbs 22:6
Philippians 1:3-6, 9-11

Example of Jesus:

Matthew 19:14

Daily meditation:

My older son yearned to play varsity football in high school. As a 15-year old sophomore he had the opportunity to be selected to practice with the varsity team for the playoff games. This would increase his chances of making the varsity team in the next season. The night before the candidates were to be named for the game, he confided that he had prayed that the Lord would use him as He saw fit and if football was how God would use him, my son would consider it a great blessing.

I too had prayed God would use my son, but when I prayed I had not known of his attitude toward God. I was doubly blessed at God's call for my son and his testimony to do the Lord's will, whatever it was.

When my son was named to play, my youngster gave the credit to the Lord and humbly thanked his Savior for the opportunity. What an experience for his mother. What a mighty God we serve!

Prayer of my heart:

Dear Lord, thank You for Your will in our lives and for the growth in my son. May he always be near to You. In Your mighty Name. Amen.

Points to ponder:

What do you learn from children? How child-like is your faith in Jesus?

Jesus was a Learner, too

Topic of the day: learner

Definition: one who discovers or comes to know, develops the habit of, becomes educated

Words from the scriptures:

Ecclesiastes 7:23-24
Proverbs 6:20-23

Example of Jesus:

Luke 2:49-52

Daily meditation:

When I think back over my experiences as a high school teacher, the most important question that runs through my mind is, "What did my students learn from me?" I wonder if they knew I loved them. Did I demonstrate the love of the Lord in all I said and did?

Learning is a vital part of our lives. We learn as toddlers how to walk and talk. We learn as children how to read and make decisions. As teens we learn independence and self-motivation. We learn how to drive a car, do our jobs, and interact with others. We meet the Lord and He teaches us what is good and evil and how to love one another.

Jesus wants to be our Teacher. Jesus wants us to learn to follow Him. Just as Jesus did the Father's will, He wants us to do the same. What are you learning from Him?

Prayer of my heart:

Jesus, thank You for showing us how to learn. Help us to be life-long learners of Your will and Your word. In Your Name we pray. Amen.

Points to ponder:

What's the most important thing you ever learned? Who was the best teacher you ever had? What are you learning today?

Foreign Language

Topic of the day: language

Definition: the expression of ideas with words

Words from the scriptures:

Psalm 19:3-4
Matthew 19:25-26

Example of Jesus:

Matthew 19:16-24

Daily meditation:

Have you ever had a conversation with someone and felt you were speaking a different language? Neither of you could get your point across to the other. So you tried a different approach and used more emphatic speech and so it went. And you went away, both disappointed and frustrated, feeling you'd lost somehow.

I wonder if that is how the Lord felt when the rich young ruler turned to leave. More importantly, how many times have I failed to comprehend what the Lord is showing *me* in His word and I turn away and sin.

Prayer of my heart:

Forgive me, Lord, for failing to understand Your messages. Thank You for continuing with me even if we don't seem to speak the same language. In Jesus' Name. Amen.

Points to ponder:

Have you ever been misunderstood? What was your reaction? Do you ever misunderstand others? What do you do about it?

Contentment

Topic of the day: contentment

Definition: to be pleased, satisfied, willing; satisfaction

Words from the scriptures:

Psalm 34:18-22
2 Corinthians 4:8-9
1 Peter 5:7-10
Philippians 4:11
1 Corinthians 13:6, 13

Example of Jesus:

Matthew 5:5

Daily meditation:

I spent many years of my life feeling like "I have no idea how to be content. I seldom feel at peace in this world." It was only by the grace of Almighty God that I didn't feel total, absolute paranoia. But as I talked with other Christians I found we all suffered from different degrees of the same affliction; we all faced fears of some sort.
My fears included questions about the success of my parenting skills, would my children be safe and find jobs? There were fears about my

financial problems in light of the changing economic times we lived in. Would I have enough money to live on if I lived to retire and if I didn't live that long, would my family be able to survive without me? Fear about my mistakes in witnessing to non-Christians I work with. Had I said or done the wrong thing and driven them away from salvation?

As we seek to know God He opens doors to let in the light of love and that love gives us security to know that God is still in control. And I am still convinced, even in the midst of my own personal fears, that love can overcome all things if God is at the heart of that love. I was not alone in my fears but God could handle them all.

Prayer of my heart:

Master of the universe, Who still loves me, be the Guide for all my actions and wipe away all my fears. Thank You for Your constant love. In Jesus, Whom I trust completely. Amen.

Points to ponder:

What do you fear? What can you do to overcome that fear? Have you trusted the Lord to manage all your fears and circumstances? If not, why not do it now?

Just Hangin' On

Topic of the day: comfort

Definition: to encourage, help, and strengthen

Words from the scriptures:

Psalm 60:11-61:3
Psalm 37:24

Example of Jesus:

John 15:5

Daily meditation:

I once saw a poster with a cat clinging to a suspended rope. The caption said, "When you reach the end of your rope tie a knot and hang on." How often I am like that foolish cat depending on a rope rather than reaching for the suspended Hands of the One in whom I trust.

In times of despair, when I am convinced I can take absolutely no more from disobedient children, despondent friends, or disappointing job pressures, what a comfort I find in Jesus and how thankful I am He holds me up.

Prayer of my heart:

O God, thank You for Your loving kindness. Help me to keep my eyes on You, O Lord. Amen.

Points to ponder:

What causes you to "reach the end of your rope?" In those instances what do you do? Do you trust Jesus with all the events of your life?

Immanuel: God With Us

Topic of the day: Immanuel or Emmanuel

Definition: Jesus Christ, especially the Messiah

Words from the scriptures:

Isaiah 7:13-14
Matthew 1:22-23
1 Corinthians 3:16

Example of Jesus:

Luke 4:16-21

Daily meditation:

Have you ever wondered why God, through His Holy Spirit, would want to know you? The idea that I am important to God and Jesus loves me has been a difficult one for me. In our humanness and with our limited minds this is a difficult concept. I have come to the conclusion that it is only through faith that we can begin to comprehend this love. The author of Hebrews tells us that without faith it is impossible to please God and He rewards those who seek Him (Hebrews 11:6). As we seek Him He reveals Himself to us and we can know Him.

Unless we are willing to look for God we will not find Him. But if we open ourselves to Him (Revelation 3:20) He will abide with us. Immanuel, God with us, residing with us, and guiding us every step of our lives.

Prayer of my heart:

Lord, I want to know You more. I want to be so close to You that You shine through all I do so the world will see You. In Jesus' Name. Amen.

Points to ponder:

Who do you know best? Who knows you best? How did that relationship come about? Do you know Jesus as well as you know that person? Why not? How can you know Jesus better?

How Well Do I Know God?

Topic of the day: longing

Definition: strong, persistent desire or craving, especially for something distant

Words from the scriptures:

Psalm 10:17
Psalm 42:1

Example of Jesus:

John 10:10

Daily meditation:

How well do I know God? Do I know Him well enough to tell Him how I feel: To share the frustrations and disappointments I experience? Do I know Him well enough to share my desires and dreams? To tell Him what I truly long for in my life? Do I know Him well enough to cry out to Him when I've reached the end of my fragile endurance? Do I know Him well enough to trust Him with my whole life? To surrender my will to His knowing He can make me complete? If not, why not?

Prayer of my heart:

Holy God, I yearn for a deeper relationship with You. May Your Holy Spirit lead me to it. In the Name of Jesus. Amen.

Points to ponder:

Where am I in my walk with the Lord? Do I long to know Him more each day? What am I doing about it? What about you? Are you where you want to be in your walk with Christ? What do you need to do to improve that situation?

In the Dark

Topic of the day: light

Definition: daytime brightness, illumination; exposure to truth

Words from the scriptures:

Genesis 1:3-4
Isaiah 2:5

Example of Jesus:

Matthew 5:14-15
Matthew 6:22-23

Daily meditation:

I walked into my son's darkened room and tripped over "something" on the floor. Although it was morning and there was some cloudy sunlight outside, the drawn drapes didn't allow the light to penetrate the room. Since I didn't bother to open the drape or flip on the overhead light I stumbled over the debris in the room before I located the items I sought.

This situation reminded me of my spiritual life. God created the sunlight to brighten the earth, light the way, and cause our necessary food to grow. God also provided Christ for us—the Light of the world—to guide us in life. But the Guide is only available if we open the drapes of our hearts and let that Light come in. Without the Light we stumble over a myriad of rubble in our paths—sin, temptation, apathy. We can flip on the switch or open the drapes with our prayers at any time. We can have our paths Lighted by the eternal Light of the world and be prevented from being engulfed by the darkness of the world if only we will open the drape and let the Light come in. Won't you do that now?

Prayer of my heart:

Jesus, my Light, guide me every step of the way as I walk through this world. Thank You for being my Beacon. In Your Name I pray. Amen.

Points to ponder:

What are you stumbling over? Have you opened your life to the Light of Jesus Christ? If not, why don't you invite Him into your life right now so He can light your pathway through the darkness? What's stopping you?

Gratitude

Topic of the day: gratitude

Definition: the feeling of being thankful

Words from the scriptures:

Psalm 147:1, 7-11

Example of Jesus:

Matthew 5:12

Daily meditation:

What are you grateful for this season? After all, Christ came to save you and me from all our sins. Shouldn't we be glad and rejoice? I struggle with a gratitude problem. In my heart I sometimes believe I earned this or I'm entitled to that or I'm simply not happy this is here or that is happening. Why should I be happy?

How often do we thank our Lord for all He does for us? Even at times when we aren't actively seeking His support for something God is at work weaving the events of our lives together for our best and His glory. God protects our children and us, provides for our personal needs—health, jobs, finances. He grants our prayer requests and loves us through our mistakes.

Today we join our lives with Biblical characters like David who thanked God for His watchful care and salvation from his deepest sin; with Rahab who was grateful for deliverance when all the rest of her town was destroyed as Jericho fell. We can relate to Paul who was glad to share the Gospel message even behind prison bars. We share in thanks with those around the world who are persecuted for worshiping the Savior, but who persevere in the midst of trials. How self-centered I have become. Forgive me, Lord. Help me to rejoice and be thankful.

What are you grateful for this season?

Prayer of my heart:

Lord Jesus, I seek your forgiveness for my unthankful heart. May Your Holy Spirit guide my wayward attitude and help me to rejoice in all the blessings You give me, every day. In the Name that is above all names, Jesus. Amen.

Points to ponder:

What causes you to be ungrateful? What makes you grateful? What makes the difference? What are you grateful for today?

Search for God's Wisdom

Topic of the day: wisdom

Definition: ability to make good use of knowledge; ability to recognize right from wrong; good judgment

Words from the scriptures:

Psalm 111:10
Proverbs 9:1-5
Hosea 14:9

Example of Jesus:

Luke 2:52

Daily meditation:

Solomon is generally accepted as the wisest man who ever lived. His wisdom was granted to him by God (1 Kings 4:29). He was also given discernment in his ability to use that wisdom. Solomon was not perfect and his decisions were not always what we might consider to be wise ones.

Our decisions can be wise only when we seek the Lord's leading. He alone can give us the ability to make good judgments in our lives.

When we try to forge ahead in our own strength often the things we become involved in or the actions we take cause us or others grief. We can increase in wisdom only as we walk with God and let Him show us the way we should go.

Prayer of my heart:

Wisdom is granted only by You, oh God. Help me to rely on You to grow in wisdom that I may make good judgments as I seek to model Jesus' love. In His Name. Amen.

Points to ponder:

Have you ever made a "wise" decision? How did you know it was wise? Do you know people you consider to be wise? What sets them apart from others? How can you increase your wisdom?

God First

Topic of the day: first

Definition: being before all others with respect to time, order, rank, importance

Words from the scriptures:

Exodus 20:2-6
Matthew 6:19-24

Example of Jesus:

Matthew 6:33

Daily meditation:

Is God really first in my life? Do I seek Him before I desire anything else on a routine day-to-day basis? Is that what it takes to be guided by His Holy Spirit in our lives and do we thwart all things if we don't do it that way? Is it realistic to pursue God first in the modern day hustle and bustle of life? Is that what God really wants? How do we know; how do we do that?

Christ said, "seek ye first the kingdom of God." (Matthew 6:33) Did He mean that literally? How did He mean for us to do that and still get everything else done? One thing I know, if God said it, He meant it, and I must do it. Scripture doesn't lie. If God isn't in first place, He is not in any place in our lives. How He achieves first place in each life is unique and purposeful for that individual, but we have to yield to Him and want Him to be, earnestly seeking Him, before He can do it.

Prayer of my heart:

Lord, I want You to be first in my life, every day. Help me as only You can. And I will give You all the praise and glory for all of my life. In Jesus' Name. Amen.

Points to ponder:

Do you want Jesus to have first place in your life? Have you confessed this to Him? What must you change to seek Him first?

God Fights For Us

Topic of the day: battles

Definition: to work very hard or struggle; strive; participation in hostile encounters or engagements

Words from the scriptures:

Nehemiah 4:20
Psalm 35:1-3
1 John 2:12-14

Example of Jesus:

John 17:14-15

Daily meditation:

In Nehemiah in the Old Testament story of the rebuilding of the wall of Jerusalem, many factions tried to interrupt the successful completion of this task. Nehemiah armed his workers and, his job done, relied on God to fight the battles.

This reminds me of my Christian walk. There are temptations to stray from the path Jesus sets before me. There are pressures to belong to the world and perform how the world performs. But if I will remember that Christ already won the war and that I am armed with His power, all I am required to do is to rely on Him to fight each battle on my behalf. Then will my joy be overflowing and the victory will bring glory to the Father.

Prayer of my heart:

Dear Lord, continue to remind me that You are in charge of my life, You fight each battle so I don't need to. Thank You for winning the war for me. In Your Name. Amen.

Points to ponder:

What battles are you fighting today? Are you winning? Why not claim the victory Christ gives you as you surrender to His will for your life?

Get Back in the Game

Topic of the day: protection

Definition: to shield from danger

Words from the scriptures:

Psalm 5:11
Psalm 40:11

Example of Jesus:

Luke 18:7-8

Daily meditation:

Life is often full of challenges. Things happen that cause us grief like the loss of a loved one or our children don't do what we expect of them. Sometimes circumstances change the security in our lives such as if we lose our jobs or are forced to relocate to keep a job. We can react to any of these life-changing events in many ways. We can become depressed or dissatisfied. We can complain or blame others or even be angry with God. Too often when disappointment or sadness enters our lives we check out or turn our backs on the Word God has directed us to.

In order to be used by God we must be available, even in the distressing times of our lives or perhaps especially in those times. We must allow God to bring us out of our focus on ourselves in our painful circumstances. We must get back in the game to complete the task set before us. The Lord will protect us through anything we face. Will we be faithful to run the race as He directs our steps?

Prayer of my heart:

Faithful and loving Father, thank You for providing a way to move through the down times as we focus on You. Hold us close as You guide us on the way You want us to go. I pray in the mighty Name of Jesus. Amen.

Points to ponder:

What circumstances are you facing that cause you to take your eyes off Christ? Who is watching how you react to negative events in your life? What example are you providing for them? Is there something you want to change in your reactions? Have you asked Jesus to help you?

Crisis Time

Topic of the day: crisis

Definition: a stage in a sequence of events at which the trend of all future events, especially for better or for worse, is determined; turning point; a condition of instability or danger, as in social, economic, political, or international affairs, leading to a decisive change; a dramatic emotional or circumstantial upheaval in a person's life.

Words from the scriptures:

Psalm 34:10
Psalm 37:4-8, 23-29

Example of Jesus:

John 3:16-21

Daily meditation:

I am continually reminded of the awesomeness of God through the ways in which He meets my needs. I have begun to realize in my life that I become practically unteachable unless I am in a crisis situation. So God gives me one "crisis" after another in order to prove my dependence on Him and to improve my relationship with Him. If I become comfortable, I tend to become complacent toward God.

In order to be used of the Lord I must not be a lukewarm Christian. For this reason the Lord allows challenges in my life that force me to grow. My prayer is that when I face, and with His help, handle these "crisis" situations others may see faith and come to know Christ.

Prayer of my heart:

My Father, thank You for meeting my needs and leading me where You want me to go. In Jesus' Name. Amen.

Points to ponder:

Do you have a crisis in your life? How are you handling it? Do you seek Jesus first and trust Him in every part of your life? Or do you insist on depending on yourself? Which works best?

Dead to self

Topic of the day: self

Definition: a person or thing referred to with respect to complete individuality

Words from the scriptures:

Psalm 5:8-10

Example of Jesus:

Matthew 23:24-26

Daily meditation:

"Lord, I want to be your servant, to be of service to the kingdom." An urgent prayer uttered frequently and with honest desire.

Jesus asks, "What are you willing to give up, to sacrifice?" An unexpected request.

"Well, surely you don't mean for me to give up the good life, my car, house, family, friends, and career?"

That is exactly what He means. "Take up your cross daily" means adjusting my attitude and activities to be in line with His. He must be first—I am to be dead to sin and self and be alive in Him. What must I do now? The choice is mine.

Prayer of my heart:

Almighty God, forgive me for my selfishness and unholy attitude. May I be willing to follow You wherever You lead me daily. Amen.

Points to ponder:

What do you cleave to today that interferes with your walk with the Lord? What is more important to you than Jesus? How does it show in your life? What do you need to do to put Jesus first in your life right now?

Convinced

Topic of the day: convince

Definition: to move by argument or evidence to belief, agreement, consent, or a course of action; to persuade

Words from the scriptures:

Revelation 3:1-6, 20-22

Example of Jesus:

Luke 20:1-8

Daily meditation:

I seldom think that what I do is so bad that the Lord will "spit me out" (Revelation 3:16) but the scripture is clear. If my walk with the Lord becomes mundane or apathetic He is not first in my life. If He is not first in my life, He is not satisfied with my relationship and I shouldn't be either. The examples of the churches in Revelation serve as examples of different relationships with the Lord. Where do I find myself?

Am I paying attention to where the Lord is leading? Have I been a faithful steward of the things He has entrusted to me—my time, money, talents? Are my actions speaking louder than my words and the broadcast says nothing about how important Jesus is in my life? I need to rethink my attitude about each activity and not be satisfied with anything I do unless Jesus is at the heart of it. How can I show others Jesus is important if my life doesn't demonstrate it? My actions have to be examples of what my words portray. Others watch us more often than they listen to us. And even if no one is watching, Jesus is. What are we saying about Jesus? What do we want to say? Jesus has first place in my life, or does He?

Prayer of my heart:

Lord, I don't want to be like the religious leaders of Jesus day or like the lukewarm believers described in Revelation. I want to be on fire for You. I want You to be first in my life, every day. Help me, Jesus. In Your Name. Amen.

Points to ponder:

Do you believe what you say you believe? How does it show? Do your actions show you are convinced that Jesus is first in your life? What do you need to change? How can you start today?

Conversations

Topic of the day: communication

Definition: the imparting or interchange of thoughts, opinions, or information by speech, writing, or signs.

Words from the scriptures:

1 Kings 18:21-39
Psalm 34:4

Example of Jesus:

John 9:36-38

Daily meditation:

During a conversation with my teenaged son he commented that his friend couldn't talk to his parents "like I can talk to you." I was reminded then of the story of Elijah and Baal's temple. The priests of Baal called on him over and over and he never responded. He couldn't. How like that example are our thwarted relationships sometimes. We simply can't communicate effectively. That sometimes includes our communications with our Heavenly Father. If we have unconfessed sin or unresolved conflicts with others, our prayers can be ineffective. We can resolve that by confession and return to a right relationship with God.

Unfortunately those who do not worship the Almighty, one true and living, God can't talk to their Parent like we believers can. They get a response like the priests of Baal, silence. They miss the calming peace only Christ can bring to a life.

May we communicate with people in such a way that they will want to know our Savior so they too can talk to God.

Prayer of my heart:

Heavenly Father, thank You for accepting relationships with us through Christ our Savior and for communicating with each of us personally. Amen.

Points to ponder:

What makes it difficult to communicate with other people? What makes it difficult to communicate with God? How can you change that?

Carrying Out Your Word
or Follow Through

Topic of the day: follow through

Definition: to continue forward to accomplish a goal or complete a task assigned

Words from the scriptures:

John 12:12-19
Colossians 3:23-24

Example of Jesus:

Luke 9:23-27

Daily meditation:

What part of the crowd are you? As Jesus rode into Jerusalem on that day we now call Palm Sunday the crush of people around Him included worshippers, close friends and the Pharisees.

From Palm Sunday to crucifixion Friday the crowd went from singing praises to crying curses toward Jesus. Even His closest friends, James, John, and Peter couldn't stay awake to pray with

Him in Gethsemane as He prayed in anguish for what was to come. They didn't follow through on their commitment to our Lord.

But Jesus did what He said He would do. He followed through on the cross. He sacrificed Himself as the Passover Lamb on the cross of Calvary. He rose again. He conquered the grave that we might be reconciled to God. We are forgiven. Celebrate. It's never too late to follow God's call.

Prayer of my heart:

Lord Jesus, thank You for Your sacrifice for me. Thank You for the opportunity to follow You and be called Your friend. Amen.

Points to ponder:

What do you have trouble following through to completion? Projects, plans for visiting friends, sending cards to the sick, other things that are important to you at one point but do not remain your focus as busyness takes over? Jesus gives us an example to adhere to for many things in scripture. It is our responsibility to carry out what He has called us to accomplish. How are you doing?

Firmer Ground

Topic of the day: foundation

Definition: base on which something is built

Words from the scriptures:

Ephesians 2:19-22

Example of Jesus:

Matthew 7:24-29

Daily meditation:

Walking on what I thought was packed snow, I suddenly fell through and created a hole in the snow. It was difficult to pull my foot out. Then I wasn't sure where a safe place was to set my foot for the next step. I spotted a rock sticking part of the way out of the snow. When I reached it I could see the firmness of its foundation on the earth.

I was reminded of the words to an old hymn. "On Christ the solid rock I stand; all other ground is sinking sand." In my life so often I become sidetracked from my focus on Christ. There seem to be so many frustrations and problems and so few apparent "rewards." Sometimes it seems God is so far away. The sand or snow allows me to sink. But when I seek out my Rock and go to Him with whatever is my concern I am lifted back onto the Foundation of my life, safe and secure in Christ.

Some people build their lives on money or fame. Some find their careers or having fun provide the foundations of what is dear to them. The only sure Foundation for our lives is Christ. His offer of life eternal is made to all. Nothing in this life should shake us off the foundation of trust in Him.

Prayer of my heart:

Thank You, Lord, for always being there to lift me up and for allowing me to build my life on such a sure Foundation. In Christ's Name. Amen.

Points to ponder:

What is your life's foundation? What shakes your foundation? Why?

Encouraging the Discouraged

Topic of the day: encouragement

Definition: to strengthen or stimulate

Words from the scriptures:

Isaiah 41:4-13
Hebrews 10:19-25
Colossians 2:2
Psalm 42:8

Example of Jesus:

Luke 12:1-7

Daily meditation:

It has been my privilege over years of Christian fellowship to pray for those close to me and for those in need of a touch from the Master. I found it easy to pray and ask God to help and protect these people.

One day I realized that, while nothing can replace our prayers, there was more to offering encouragement and giving support to others than praying for them. I could phone a friend, personally visit the sick, or babysit so someone could go shopping. I could write a letter or send a card to one in pain.

When fellow Christians need me, I still pray first; but now I try to offer more tangible support too.

Prayer of my heart:

Dear Lord, thank You for hearing our prayers and allowing us to be encouragers to those who are discouraged. Thank You for Your constant encouragement and the Example You set for us. Amen.

Points to ponder:

What was the greatest encouragement you ever received? From whom did it come? How did it make you feel? What kind of an encourager are you? Who do you need to encourage today?

Relax in Jesus

Topic of the day: relax

Definition: to make less tense, rigid, or firm

Words from the scriptures:

Romans 13:14
Romans 7:14-25
Galatians 5:16-25

Example of Jesus:

John 6:40
John 14:6
John 16:33

Daily meditation:

Remember how it feels to strain to accomplish some physical activity? It hurts. Then you take a hot shower or bath and the muscles relax and the pain is eased. We strain in our spiritual activities also, as we, like Paul, struggle with the flesh. We want to serve Jesus as believers but we just can't seem to accomplish it. Our flesh intrudes. So we either give up, or become frustrated in our fleshly attempts. However, we forget the promise God gave us.

God sent us Jesus so we could be saved from our flesh and its sinful nature. We have been transformed, given a new nature. Because we have flesh we are determined to do things ourselves. God's plan is for us to let Him do whatever is to be accomplished through His Holy Spirit. So relax in Jesus. Let Him do it. Do not be concerned about the flesh for the Lord has overcome it.

Prayer of my heart:

Holy Lord, thank You for overcoming my desires in the flesh and working through the Holy Spirit to accomplish Your purposes in my life. Help me to cede my desires to You and relax knowing You are in charge. In that matchless Name, Jesus. Amen.

Points to ponder:

What causes you concern? What problem you encounter is too big for Jesus to handle? Why can't you relax in the arms of Jesus?

Along Comes Jesus

Topic of the day: Jesus

Definition: the source of the Christian religion, also called Jesus Christ, Jesus of Nazareth

Words from the scripture:

Luke 24:13-16

Example of Jesus:

Luke 24:25-26, 30-31

Daily meditation:

Along comes Jesus in the breaking of the bread.
Along comes Jesus, to turn my head, to lead me to the place where I can know my need for the Father's only Son.
Empowered by His grace, all-knowing and all-loving, to know Him only, always, in the breaking of the bread.

Messiah, Adonai, Holy Son of God, sacrificed for my sin, Who came to me through the cross at Calvary. Into my heart you came, to give me a brand new start, to be known by me in the breaking of the bread.

Prayer of my heart:

Lord Jesus, reveal Yourself anew to me and others as You did to those on the road to Emmaus. Open our eyes that we may see clearly what it is You are teaching us today. In Your Name, Amen.

Points to ponder:

Who do you think Jesus is? Is He your Savior and Lord? Do you know Him personally? Do you want to know Him more?

Will the Real Jesus Please Stand Up?

Topic of the day: authentic, real

Definition: not false or copied; genuine; having the origin supported by unquestionable evidence, authenticated, verified; true

Words from the scriptures:

Philippians 2:5-8
John 1:1-5, 14
Matthew 2:4-6
Matthew 26:26-28

Example of Jesus:

John 2:1-11

Daily meditation:

There was a television program from my childhood that questioned people who all claimed to be the same person. The panel was allowed to ask questions then vote on who they believed to be the person they all claimed to be. Only one could be authentic and at the end of the program the announcer would say, "Will the real (whoever it was named) please stand up?"

This program now reminds me of the challenges the world presents to the True and Living Christ. The world now questions Christmas and all it represents. It asks if the baby born in a manger in Bethlehem is the real Jesus. The child who lingered in the temple talking with the teachers in Jerusalem, was this twelve-year old boy the real Jesus? Is the real Jesus the man who turned the water into wine at a wedding feast in Cana? Was the real Jesus the One the devil tempted in the wilderness? Or was He the One who cleared the temple of the money changers?

Could the real Jesus be the One who healed the sick, made the lame to walk and the blind to see and even raised the dead to life? Did the real Jesus eat the bread and drink the wine at supper and one day die on the cross of Calvary? Did He pray with His disciples for the world, for you and me? Why would the real Jesus do all that and much, much more?

This is all true about the Real Jesus Who came from heaven to earth to be the sacrifice on Calvary. He died to make us free, to provide salvation for you and me. He calls to each of us, reaching out in love, to look and see this is the Real Jesus meant to be the Perfect Lamb on Calvary's tree. The Real Jesus stood up to give to me His peace and joy if on Him I will rely.

So I offer this Happy Birthday, Jesus, as I stand up for Him today. I will acknowledge Him as Lord and tell the world the Real Jesus came to Bethlehem. He came to you and me on Christmas sent from God above so we can have eternal life because of His great love.

Prayer of my heart:

No words can ever express the love you gave to all mankind in the form or a human baby born that Christmas morn. So we will give

You what You want from us, dear Lord. We give ourselves as our Christmas gift to You. Thank You, Jesus. Amen.

Points to ponder:

Who do you believe Jesus is? Is He your Savior and Lord? What will you do to keep Him in Christmas this year and all the year through?

Bibliography

Amplified Cross-reference Bible. Grand Rapids, Mich: Zondervan, 2014. Print.

"BibleGateway." .com: A Searchable Online Bible in over 100 Versions and 50 Languages. N.p., n.d. Web. From 27 April 2011 till 11 Apr. 2015. <https://www.biblegateway.com/>. (translations used include: New Living Translation, New King James Version, King James Version, New International Version, The Message, Amplified Bible, New American Standard Bible, Amplified Bible, Classic Edition, Living Bible)

Dictionary.com. Dictionary.com, n.d. Web. 2011-2015. <http://dictionary.reference.com/>.

"What a Friend We have in Jesus" hymn by Joseph Scriven 1855.

Yager, Elisa. "Morning Coffee With Jesus—December 2, 2009." Hub Pages Inc. 2011 Retrieved from bing April 27, 2011

<http://hubpages.com/hub/Morning-Coffee-with-Jesus-December-2-2009>.

About the Author

The author is a Christ follower who has dedicated her life to teaching others. With a Bachelor of Arts degree in history and a master's degree in education the author was involved in curriculum writing throughout her career as a teacher. She was a public high school teacher for 35 years in California then moved to Idaho to teach junior and senior high school students at a private Christian school. Since retiring from classroom teaching the author has enjoyed meeting with Bible study groups in the community and her local church both as a teacher and as a learner.

The author enjoys traveling around the country especially visiting historical sites. When she is not writing, she quilts, studies scriptures, and reads both fiction and non-fiction books.

The author has been blessed by a loving and supportive family that includes two grown sons and three grandsons as well as a large extended family and friends around the country. She currently lives on the family farm in Idaho.

Printed in the United States
By Bookmasters